And in due time Hannah conceived and bore a son

and she called his name Samuel, for she said, "I

have asked for him from the LORD."

1 Samuel 1:20

Chloe's Gift

Lost is Found

To Karen, Clay, Bess and Sam

And all the pets they've loved:

Fancy, Meg, Oscar, Big Kitty, Kitty, Annie, Tootsie,

Huckleberry, Chloe, Mr. Kitten, Penelope,

Brother, Bella, Fiona, Longfellow, Oakley, and of

course The Big Guy-Rocky.

Chloe's Gift

Author: John McHugh

"Long-suffering" ear: Karen McHugh

Jennie Cooper Press

ISBN: 978-0-9886618-0-6

March 2014

Table of Contents

Chapter One - Meg

John, a doctor, receives a phone call at his office. It was his wife Karen.

"John, I have decided to put Meg to sleep. The vet is coming at lunch to give the shot. If you want to be here, we are doing it then. I cannot bear to see her like this anymore."

John left work after his last morning patient and arrived at his home as the veterinarian was leaving. She offered a pleasantly restrained yet compassionate smile as they passed each other.

"Your wife is up in the woods," she said pointing to an area of trees at the edge of the garden.

Meg had been sick for months now. She had an abdominal cancer, which was not operable, and had been slowly losing weight despite her belly increasing in girth. John and Karen had debated for weeks about the timing of putting her to sleep, but had not reached a consensus about when, where, or how to do it. Karen elected to take matters in her own hands.

When John arrived at the spot in the woods alluded to by the vet, Karen was sitting with Meg. Meg had the appearance of sleeping comfortably in Karen's lap. There was a shaved spot on Meg's front leg with an I.V. in it. As he approached it became clear the Vet had already injected the life ending medicine. Meg was motionless and Karen was crying. Karen crying was as gut wrenching to him as it was seeing Meg lifeless. He instinctively knew and felt the emotional rollercoaster Karen had been through that morning and now was experiencing the same thing.

"I am so sorry John. I could not look at her anymore. I don't think it has been fair to her. I hope you don't feel I have been unfair to you. The time had come. Please don't be disappointed in me for doing this."

John said nothing. His eyes moistened as he sat down next to Karen and began to stroke Meg's hair; that familiar, soft, and beautiful golden hair which was so characteristic of their beloved golden retriever. It was the same hair which John, Karen, and their three children cuddled in time and time again and had come to love for over fourteen years.

After about thirty minutes of silence and the rush of memories that filled both of their hearts, John said, "You go in and I'll bury her." He had started digging the hole to bury Meg in several weeks ago. The spot was just a bit further into the woods from where they were sitting and the reason Karen chose that particular spot to end Meg's suffering.

Karen said, "I can help you."

"That's okay, I finished the hole last night, and I would like some time alone with her as well," John said.

He put Meg in a large trash bag which he had put in the grave days before and very carefully and lovingly placed her in the grave. He positioned her in the bag and placed her head in such a way as to protect her beautiful face from the weight of the forthcoming earth.

The first dirt he placed on Meg he did with his hands being careful not to let it land directly on her head or where he thought her eyes would be. Once Meg was completely covered in dirt, he then used the shovel to complete the task. He took the rocks that he'd collected over the last several weeks in anticipation of this day and spelled "MEG" on the top of the grave. He then sat alone. Quietly, while remembering all she had meant to him and his family, he wept.

Chapter Two-A dog shows up at the lake

John and Karen had two other dogs, Oscar and Tootsie, both of whom they loved dearly, but there was an emptiness around their home without Meg. The couple felt her memory and presence everywhere in and about the house. The couch, the trampoline, the backyard, the bedroom, the children's rooms, the porch, and years and years of pictures with members of the family framed throughout the house, served as a constant reminder of Meg. The two remaining dogs were dachshunds; Oscar was the grouchy father, and Tootsie, a high maintenance daughter. The female dachshund next door had been Oscar's wife and Tootsie's mother. It had been an "arranged" marriage.

"I miss having a big dog around here John," Karen said.

"I miss having a dog that likes being in water," John replied. He thought, "Dachshunds are like cats, they do not like water and don't swim."

John and Karen had a small piece of property on the lake near their home. They rarely spent the night at the small cabin on the site, but very much enjoyed going there for "day trips" and always got home before the time the street lights came on.

John and Meg could easily consume a Saturday at the lake with cutting grass, fishing, and working in their small garden there. They often visited the big box stores for stuff needed for whatever they would be doing that day. Meg loved riding in John's truck, ambling around the property, and dipping into the lake for a swim from time to time as John worked.

"John, what on earth do you and Meg do all day out there?" Karen often asked.

John and Meg looked at Karen in unison and agreed that Karen just did not "get it."
"Well Karen, Meg and me don't have nothing to do out there, we got all day to do it, and we may not get but half of it done," John answered. He wasn't sharing any of their secrets.

With Meg gone there was a void on Saturdays, not only at home for the couple, but also for John at the lake. John attempted to make the dachshunds his "lake dogs," but they did not like water and just made a mess out of his Saturdays. Oscar hated it at the lake preferring the warm and known confines of their home and being a lovable grouch on his turf. Tootsie loved riding in the truck to the lake and she loved to cuddle in the warmth of John's jacket during the ride however, Tootsie was always doing something meddlesome. She explored to the extent that John spent the majority of his time looking for her or keeping Tootsie out of trouble.

On one occasion John lost Tootsie for about two hours though it seemed like an eternity. During the time she was missing, he frantically searched the shore of the lake, the cabin, and the surrounding area. He envisioned Karen chastising him for not "taking better care of Tootsie." All of his worst fears as to her safety ran through his mind only to find her on top of the boat dock. Tootsie had no problem climbing the steps to the top of the deck, but once there, she would not come back down. He found her accidentally because he saw the silhouette of her small head on the horizon of the dock flooring. His fear of finding the more worrisome silhouette of her body floating in water hence relinquished, John commenced to chastise her under his breath. (Tootsie's head is small for her body. John's head is small and Karen often made fun of him for it. John's mother said her first memory of John as a baby was that he could, "cover his whole face with his hand." On his high school football team in LaGrange,

Georgia, he wore the smallest helmet. It was a size 6 and 7/8, and was specially ordered for him. Karen told John, when she perceived he was gaining weight, "John, you need to be careful about gaining too much weight or you'll start looking like Tootsie. Your head won't match your body.")

On another fateful day at the lake, Tootsie chased a mouse or some other rodent under the cabin, which had only a six-inch crawl space, and it took several hours to determine where she was. Once found, she would not come out and there was no obvious way to get to her or to get her out. Complicating the situation and intensifying the anxiety for John, it was not clear if Tootsie was trapped or just would not come out. Exasperated and about to give up, John found a neighbor with a skill saw to cut a hole in the cabin's kitchen floor to "rescue" her. The sawed out square of flooring replaced the hole in a patch-like fashion serving as a constant reminder of that day's three-hour ordeal to free Tootsie from the confines of the cabin crawlspace.

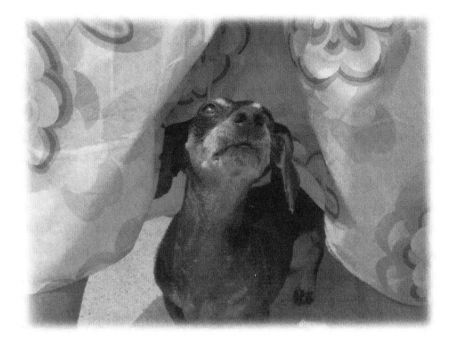

"Karen, I am not taking Tootsie out to the lake anymore. She is a good truck dog and likes to ride, but she is way too much trouble for me out there. I can't get anything done with her. She gets into stuff. "Dachshunds have a Napoleon complex and that's her problem," John thought. He, however, did take her again. It would be a mistake to do so, and it would be the last trip to the lake for Tootsie.

The "last" time Tootsie went to the lake with John, she played the "Napoleon role" that only a foot-long dachshund can do with the great dane puppy which lived next door. She barked and taunted the dog until it grabbed her like a pillow, shook her, and then threw her about thirty feet. All of this transpired in a matter of seconds right in front of John to his amazement and chagrin while he was raking leaves and listening to a Georgia football game. Tootsie's run in with the great dane resulted in a trip to the vet, a V-neck T-shirt soaked with Tootsie's blood, ten holes in Tootsie's abdomen (but no damage to her intestine), two hours of surgery in which John assisted the vet, fifty stitches, and another ruined Saturday at the lake. No Tootsie was not to be another Meg and she would not be going to the lake anymore, period. To make matters worse, on the day Tootsie came home from the hospital, John was holding her in his arms, and was about to give her cheek a kiss when she snapped up and bit him on the tip of his nose. He dropped her to the floor out of shock and a bit of anger, only to find her running to Karen. Karen now became the "good-guy" and Tootsie's savior in this unprovoked attack, which further aggravated John. Karen then laughed uncontrollably at the situation and particularly at John clutching his nose. John's nose was now bleeding profusely and when he checked it out in the mirror there was an inch long scratch which was deep and devoid of skin. The area subsequently scabbed over and for two weeks was a painful and visual reminder of the little ungrateful troublemaker that was Tootsie.

"Dr. McHugh, what happened to your nose?" John was asked a thousand times over the ensuing weeks.

"My dog bit me," he answered. Having to respond to that question in light of the history of the event was "salt on the wound" to John. He did, however, forgive Tootsie.

Several months later after blowing leaves at the lake, John alone and without a lake dog, was resting on an old spring swing left at the lake by the original owner of the property Jessie Jewell. He saw a small puppy walking up the gravel driveway. The lake property is at the end of a road that has a cul de sac. His first thought was that someone had dropped off the dog and left it. As the puppy approached her gait and color made John think that the visitor was a golden retriever puppy and probably one of a neighbor's dogs. She walked nonchalantly to where he was sitting and sat down right next to him. It was as if she was already his dog and that what she was doing now was what she was accustomed to doing naturally and often.

"Well, what's your name, cutie pie?" John asked somewhat taken aback by the level of the "make yourself right at home" nature of this stranger.

The dog's tail began wagging as it looked up at John contentedly. John confirmed that the dog was a female, and as best he could tell, she was a thoroughbred. He figured that someone was probably missing her pretty bad about now. She had no collar. It was unknown to John at the time that this was a foreboding sign. He picked her up, held her in his lap with her belly up, legs open and apart, and began to rub her. To John, a dog that will let you rub its belly is an "at peace" dog and a prerequisite characteristic of one you'd want to have. Oscar would not let you do that, but Tootsie would. This dog was as laid back as you please to be on her back and be rubbed, particularly behind her ears.

"I think I'll keep you my little friend. Do you like the water?"

When John and the new dog arrived home that evening, he said as he entered the house, "Karen, guess what showed up at the lake today?"

Karen immediately said, "She's pretty. Look at her tongue; it's got a black spot on it. That means she has chow in her."

"You don't know that Karen. A black spot on the tongue? Are you kidding?"

"It means she has Chow in her. I bet she is a Golden-Chow." Karen was right about the puppy having Chow in her as evidenced by the way her bushy tail always was curled up over her back. None of the neighbors near the lake cabin reported losing a dog and so the family adopted the golden retriever looking puppy with the bushy tail and black spotted tongue as their own.

Bess, their middle child who was in sixth grade at the time, named the new pet Chloe. The new dog was the same color as Meg and since Meg was named after the spice, nutmeg, Bess wanted to name her after another brownish colored spice. She thought chloe was a spice as well. That chloe was not a spice was something that John and Karen did not note, but would not have corrected it even if they had noticed the error. John, a poor speller, the next day went to PetSmart to make a tag for her collar, but spelled her name "Clohe" much to the sarcastic delight of his family who never let him forget that he spelled her name incorrectly. Named for a spice that wasn't, and having to wear a tag with the wrong name on it may have very well been a glimpse into Chloe's unpredictable future.

The couple and their family fell instantly in love with the gentle intruder. As John's mother would say, "One man's loss is another one's gain."

The "gift" and the coming saga that was Chloe then commenced; the extent and complexity of which was unknown to John or Karen at the time. Chloe on the other hand, knew exactly what was to come and the role she'd play in the lives of John, Karen, their family, and more importantly, other lives.

15 *Chloe's Gift*

Chapter Three-Chloe has layers

Chloe quickly became an integral part of her new "finders" family. As time went on, several interesting things became apparent about her. First of all, she was accident prone, both of her own accord and as a result of the unintentional actions of others. In the first year the family had her she fell off the thirty-foot high back porch and broke one of her legs. On another occasion, Karen ran over Chloe as she ran to greet her car resulting in a broken shoulder on the same side as the previously broken leg. It seemed that Chloe was perpetually in a lampshade, (that loathsome device devised by vets to keep dogs from licking and picking at the injured part of their body.) Chloe was in one of these lampshades so often that John thought he might save them to use in a business venture featuring used animal lampshades (rescued lampshades so to speak) with cute little designs on them which Karen, an artist, would draw. About the time they decided to throw away a lampshade, Chloe would re-injure herself again, and the couple found themselves having to buy yet again something they had just thrown away. Trips to the vet and the resultant lampshades were quickly making Chloe a lovable, but expensive pet. This however was only the start of it.

"I am afraid to throw away this lampshade contraption, Karen; it might be a bad luck thing to do. The minute I do she gets hurt or something, and we'll have to buy another one."

 In about the same spot where Karen ran over Chloe, one year later Karen then ran into a child in the neighborhood driving a golf cart. Chloe was with Karen, the car was totaled and the accident consequentially blamed on Chloe's bad karma. More than the fact that the child did not look both ways and pulled out in front of Karen's car, John and Karen were slowly getting the gist of Chloe. Being accident prone, however, was not Chloe's biggest issue. She was an unusual animal in many ways and often behaved more like a person than a dog.
"Chloe has layers," Karen would say adding, "She is complex."

Chloe was a pensive dog for certain and had a major problem with loud noises, particularly thunder. Thunder brought out unknown demons (they thought) in Chloe and made her very anxious. This fear of thunder resulted in her running away from home. It became a major and reoccurring problem for Chloe and consequently for her family. Chloe's fear of thunder was complicated by the fact that John and Karen, and for that matter Chloe, were not good at making sure Chloe had her collar on at all times. For various reasons, the collar would be taken off for a bath, and it would just happen that a major storm would occur the same day. The collar came off in mysterious ways as well. On one occasion it blew off Chloe's neck while she had her head out John's truck's window on the way to the Chattahoochee River some thirty miles from home. The collar was received in the mail about two weeks later. If it happened that Chloe was outside when the thunder occurred, she defaulted by running away. She ran away to various destinations. For a time she would end up at their next-door neighbor's house. The reason she went next door was because she was accustomed to going there on Sundays. Their next-door neighbor always cooked out steaks on Sunday night. Unbeknownst to her owners, Chloe disappeared on Sunday about the time these neighbors started cooking the meat. It took a while, but John and Karen began to note that during the same two-hour period each Sunday, they could not find Chloe. Chloe's absence every Sunday evening was not a point of concern. In this instance and during this particular time, they did not know where she was, but they knew she'd be back. She always resurfaced on

Sunday evenings. At a neighborhood party, John and Karen finally confirmed the location of where Chloe went on Sunday evenings.

"John, guess who came over for steaks this past Sunday?" asked his next-door neighbor.

"I don't know, Wayne, who?"
"Chloe, she loves to come over for steak. She comes in after eating and watches a few shows on the couch with my wife and me. She is so sweet. We don't need our own dog with Chloe as our neighbor. A couple of hours with Chloe on Sunday are just right for us and all we need. I'll put a couple of cute pictures in your mailbox of her watching a game with us on our couch."

The fact that Chloe was at peace with everyone she met and "took up with," did not give John and Karen any solace. In time this trait, in addition to her penchant to flee, became very problematic for the couple and complicated their ability to recover her when she ran away.

If it was raining and Karen and John heard thunder, they simultaneously thought, "Uh oh...where's Chloe?" The searching again then began in earnest. First stop would be the neighbors who cooked out the steaks on Sunday. The next stop would be the neighbors up the street who had a Beagle that Chloe played with from time to time.

"Karen, this is Neal. Chloe is up here in our garage. Do you want me to bring her down there to you?"

"Thanks Neal. No, that won't be necessary. We'll be up in a minute."

In time, the places she'd run to became more distant, and very much more complicated by the fact that at times she would not have on her collar. The primary place to which she gravitated outside the neighborhood was the grocery store about a mile from John and Karen's home. To get to this store Chloe went up the street from the couple's house to the main road, a very busy and potentially dog-lethal road, take a right, and then go about another half a mile to cross yet another busy street to end up in front of the grocery store, Ingles. The couple had no clue why she chose that place to go when it thundered. As it had happened on many occasions in the past, the phone rang at John and Karen's home at three in the morning.

"Hi, this is Bill up at Ingles. I think we have your dog up here."

"Thank you. I'll be up there in a few minutes," John replied.

John arrived and just outside the door of the store on the curb is a girl sitting and petting Chloe. Chloe seemed surprised that she was John's dog and that he was there to pick her up. As usual she had taken to the person she had ended up with and vice versa. John got out of the car, opened the passenger side door and simply said quietly, "Chloe, let's go home." She jumped up in the car seat as if it were part of the original plan. Chloe looked at John as if to say, "What's the big deal. I was fine here, leave me alone."

"She is one sweet dog," would be the obligatory remark of the Ingles employee.

"Yeah, yeah, yeah," John would think. He had heard it too many times before. It wasn't funny or cute any more. Chloe's internal mental issues and the effect they were having on her family's lives were beginning to "grate."

One of John's Saturday rituals involved going to various stores to get the things he needed for a particular project at the lake that day. After John and Chloe took the trash to the compacter, the next stop on their route was Home Depot. John found a shady parking spot a bit away from the other cars, carefully adjusted the windows for just the right ventilation, and then made it a point not to be in the store longer than fifteen minutes. One episode pertaining to a "Chloe disappearance," happened in the parking lot of a Home Depot. Chloe somehow had gotten out of the truck while John was shopping. After having looked all over the parking lot and the area around the store, a lady pulled up in a car. John saw Chloe sitting up in the passenger side of the car as if she were a family member. She looked like she was the one who owned the car, and the lady driving the car was Chloe's chauffeur. Chloe looked at John as if John was the stranger or as if he was the one who was lost and she had come to claim him. He was slowly catching on to Chloe's ways, and began to wonder, "Is there more to this dog than he or Karen realized? Could it be that Chloe had found them and not the other way around? Had she done to John and Karen what she was doing to all these other people who kept finding her?"

"Is this your dog? She followed me as I was leaving the store and got in my car. She is the sweetest dog," the finder said.

"Yes she's mine. She doesn't know a stranger alright. Thanks so much. Come on Chomplex," John said reluctantly recalling all the other episodes in which Chloe's friendliness made him look like an irresponsible master. He thought to himself, "This lady is probably thinking I was wrong to leave her in the car unattended. That poor dog was hot and I should have known you don't leave a dog in a car alone. I know exactly what she's thinking. Thanks a lot Chloe. You are as bad as Tootsie."

A variation of the above scenario easily happened twenty times over the course of the fourteen years the family lived with Chloe. Mixed in with her runaways with a collar-on, were at least ten or so runaways without a collar. The no-collar Chloe episodes were more troubling and accompanied by a larger degree of anxiety on the part of John and Karen, but the with-collar episodes were problematic as well. Not the least of these was when she followed John or Karen's car as they left on their daily affairs. John in particular worried about this type of following maneuver. John and Karen's first dog, a cockapoodle named Fancy, (named after a Rod Stewart album, they had called her "Footloose and Fancy Free"). Fancy was hit and killed by a car after following John, unbeknownst to him, on a bike ride. He did not know she had been killed until he and Karen missed her and then he backtracked his bike route and found her on a busy road he routinely crossed on his ride. He had never forgotten her death and blamed himself for it.

Chloe's habit of following the car when John or Karen left home became almost as much a frustrating issue for them as her disappearing because of thunder. If they did not make a point to let her go to the restroom, and then put her back into the house before they left, particularly if it were a rainy day, she followed the car. Dealing with this was not only time consuming, but very aggravating because it almost always occurred when either John or Karen was in a hurry or late for something. The other problem with this bad habit of Chloe's was the potential negative consequence of John or Karen not noticing that she was following them. Chloe had figured out a clever way to follow their cars by cutting through the woods adjacent to their house and then begin following their car further up the street. This was a problem because John or Karen, not seeing Chloe follow them out of the driveway, assumed she was not following. Then it was possible for her to continue following their car out of the neighborhood without their knowledge and expose herself to the busy main road. This put Chloe in danger of getting hit or began the whole running away routine all over again. "Ingles here I come," Chloe must have thought as she followed John or Karen's car out of the neighborhood.

Could it have been that she was yearning for something different in her life or to be somewhere else? Was this family just a stopping point on the journey to another more important destination for Chloe? Could it be that running away and being with others who happened to "find her" had been the very thing she wanted and yearned for all along? It was becoming very clear to John and Karen that Chloe was indeed complex, and she may have in her head another purpose in her life other than being part of theirs.

As a matter of habit John and Karen would pull out of the driveway and instinctively look into the rearview mirror to be sure that Chloe was not following. If she was, they turned around, went back to the house and then enticed her to go inside the house before either could leave. This could take several minutes. With each successive episode she became more suspicious and wise to their diversionary tactics and this made getting her in the house more difficult. In time she suspected the ploy and would not follow the car down the drive to the house, but rather wait where the driveway met the street. This too made leaving home without Chloe, if she wanted to follow, harder to do. If this happened and her "owners" were late, they were forced to let her in the car at the street and take her with them, which was most probably Chloe's original intention.

"If you are going to act this way then you can go, but you are going to have sit in the car a long time Chloe. You are going to need that basketball bladder of yours today; I have a lot to do. You are going to have to stop doing this," John would admonish her.

It is noted, however, that she did get her way. For the most part Chloe always got her way. She "owned" John and Karen. She did not own them in a pompous or pious way; she owned them in a sweet and unrequited way. John, Karen, and their children were all right with it. They loved and adored Chloe. Thinking of Chloe reminded John of a phrase his mother was fond of using to describe a person to whom everyone gave a pass and treated as if they were "entitled." "She's a prima donna, and they think she can do no wrong," his mother would say in a somewhat condescending way. It fit Chloe to a tee.

For John the most frustrating time Chloe would pull the "I'll follow your car out of the driveway trick" was on the mornings he had surgery to perform at the hospital. Perpetually tardy by nature and cutting it close time-wise on one such "surgery morning," John saw Chloe in the rear view mirror of the car as he pulled out of the driveway.

"Not again!"

Chloe's following the car was a fifteen-minute ordeal regardless of the mechanism used to deal with it. Over time John developed a technique that worked well at first, improved as Chloe got older and became increasingly afflicted by arthritis. If it were determined that he was being followed, John turned the car around and drove past his house in the opposite direction. He went very slowly to be sure that Chloe was on the safe side of the street as she followed the car. After about six or so houses beyond his home, he'd slowly turn around and then gradually gain speed and leave her. What usually happened was that about the time she got to their driveway John's car was out of sight. She gave up the chase, as it was all up hill beyond the driveway, and exhaustion trumped her desire to follow. On many occasions however, John waited at the stop sign at the junction with the main street to be sure she did make the entire journey to follow his car, which occasionally happened. She followed John's car all the way to the stop sign on many occasions, but as she got older she'd more often than not she gave up when she reached the house.

Losing Chloe because of her following John or Karen's car without their knowledge only happened a few times. When it did occur she was found either in the neighborhood or at Ingles the majority of the time. This was not as major a problem as losing her because of a storm in the middle of the night. The worst-case scenario occurred when there was a storm with thunder, her collar was off, and they were either asleep or not home.

Then there was the time that John had taken Chloe in his truck with him to make Saturday rounds at the hospital. He purposely left one of the windows down a distance to ventilate, but not enough to allow for Chloe's escape. Somehow, while John was in the hospital checking on his patients, Chloe jumped out of the truck window. It probably occurred because a dog walked by and Chloe's habit of going berserk in the confines of a car if a dog happened by. She was found by a couple of nursing students. The nurses in turn called the number on her tag and consequently John's oldest son Clay came to the hospital to get her. Clay came so promptly to pick Chloe up that John always thought it had more to do with seeing the nurses than recovering Chloe.

Anyway, John came out of the hospital about thirty minutes later to an empty truck with no Chloe. While he was trying to figure out what had happened to Chloe, since the opening in the window did not look like it would permit Chloe's squeezing out, he got a phone call on his cell.

"Dad, this is Clay. I've got Chloe. She jumped out of your truck and some nurses called me to come get her. Dad, you have got to be more careful with Chloe. She is very important to us. You can't keep losing her like this," he says.
John responded, "Thanks Clay, I'll try to do better."

These near misses with Chloe being lost then serendipitously found made John and Karen's family begin to again wonder, "Does Chloe's getting lost so often and then being found in the oddest ways have some purpose or meaning? Why does this keep happening?"

Chapter Four-No collar disappearances-the worst kind

Over the subsequent years there were several close calls in which John and Karen almost lost Chloe for good. Each time it was a happenchance occurrence in which her collar was not on and there was either a storm or a loud noise. For instance, one "no- collar" occasion happened on a July 4, a thunder-like episode in which she happened to be outside when the local fireworks show started.

Each disappearance had a similar chain of events and often began with Karen's ritual of going outside to feed the cats, saying good morning to all of the animals, and making an accounting of each. Karen did this religiously each morning. The two cats spent most of their time outside, but came in occasionally. The two dachshunds spent most of their time outside as well, came in often during the day, but slept in the garage. Chloe was in and out, but for the most part slept inside on a couch at the end of the bed in the couple's bedroom. Chloe preferred to sleep inside. If she happened to sleep outside, she knew how to paw at the front door knob and open it. She however never learned or took the time to learn shutting the front door. (This made sense to her. She was only concerned about getting in the house. It wasn't that she was lazy or not smart enough.) So, if it thundered in the night, and by chance the front door was locked and she was outside, then off she'd go. If the collar happened to be off, well, the search efforts began anew in the morning when Karen discovered Chloe was unaccounted for.

The way they figured it, Chloe first checked all the doors at her house to see if she could get in and if that failed, made her rounds of the two neighbors previously mentioned. If that did not work, off to Ingles she'd go. If the couple knew she was missing early on, Chloe could be found wandering around at the Ingles parking lot. Often they arrived at Ingles to find her playing with an employee of Ingles. If too much time elapsed or Ingles was closed, she continued on her journey. The couple never understood why Chloe would leave like that or what exactly did she have in mind. They wondered if she knew exactly what she was doing and where she was going. "She's complex," came to mind when it was determined she was gone yet again. Concern, mixed with anger directed at Chloe and at themselves, then ensued.

On each occurrence of Chloe's "gone missing" a series of events came into play. The couple checked the house, garage, above the garage, and the immediate surrounding areas in the neighborhood. The next step was to call the most common homes she'd frequent in the neighborhood and check her expected route to Ingles. This would result in successfully finding Chloe in the majority of cases.

If still missing after the initial protocol, the next step involved quizzing the employees of Ingles, or calling the Humane Society to see if they had a "golden" looking dog with a black spot on her tongue. Placing lost dog signs with her picture in and around Ingles followed. A verifying trip to the Humane Society to be sure that the description they gave of Chloe matched the one the volunteer wrote down. Walking through the maze of cages at the Humane Society is something that was done often over the years, sometimes with results, more commonly not. The people who took the time to help Chloe became attached to her and thus did not call the pound to pick her up even if that was their initial intention. It would be obvious to any helpful stranger that she was special and had been loved very much by someone. It became quickly apparent to them that she was a "keeper."

On one of the more interesting occasions Chloe had been missing for three days. A neighbor of the family was getting gas at a Citgo station adjacent to the Ingles shopping center and saw a dog in the back of a car next to his that looked like Chloe.

The phone rang and Karen picked up.
"Karen, this is David. Do ya'll have Chloe?" Everyone in the neighborhood knew of Chloe's penchant to roam.
"As a matter of fact, no, she ran off three days ago and we can't find her," she answered.

"I think I just saw her at the Citgo station near Ingles. She was in the back seat of a car that was getting gas. She was sitting with two little kids. I told the lady that I thought the dog was yours and got her number. I told her you'd be calling."

David related the lady's phone number to Karen, and she called to give the identifying features of Chloe. Once the identity was confirmed to the satisfaction of the person, directions were reluctantly given about where to come get her. As usual Chloe had adapted seamlessly to the new family and when Karen and John arrived she was rocking in a swing with children on the porch, as if she were a Cabbage Patch Doll and playing the role of the perfect pet she was. Chloe's eyes glanced over at Karen as she got out of the car and began to walk toward her. Chloe's expression intimated the now familiar question," Why are you here?"

"This is one sweet dog. We sure are going miss Sandy. That's what the children named her."

"Where did you find her?" Karen asked.

Karen knew better than to ask that question and John wished she hadn't. In all the other times in which Chloe got lost, the person who found her always had the same answer. The response, whether meant purposefully or as a Freudian slip, served as a stinging commentary as to the quality of the owners of such a wonderful and loving dog. Each time the sarcastic nature of the response was duly noted, particularly by John.

"We found her cold, hungry, and wet roaming around the parking lot of Ingles one morning. We took her home, gave her a bath and fed her. She adores attention and being loved on."

"Whatever. Spare me," John thought. "Just give me my dog back and leave off the commentary." In the car they would have the same old worn out conversation with the Chloe-miester. "Chlompie, you are going to have to stop doing this. One day we are not going to be lucky enough to find you. Let's get you home to see Oscar and Tootsie you silly dog, they've missed you. We love you Co Co, we love you so much. We need to take you to Miss Brenda for a haircut. Don't you do this to us again, you hear?"

On another occasion with a similar scenario Chloe by happenchance did not have on her collar, a storm was brewing and she couldn't get in the house because the front door was locked, so she went to Ingles. No one had seen hide nor hair of her. The day after Chloe went missing this particular time was a Thursday. John remembered the day because he and Karen always started to really worry on day three as most pounds will put unclaimed dogs to sleep after that period of time. John and Karen called the Hall County Humane Society and asked if a "golden" type dog has been found. John described Chloe as looking like a golden retriever, with a black spot on her tongue, a bushy tail, and shorter in statue than a golden would be.

"She's a golden chow, everything about her is like a golden but pudgier."

"Let me look through the roster here. No, none of the dogs we have fit that description."

"Has anyone called in and said they have found a dog that looks like my dog?"

"Let me look at the call-in sheet. Nope, nothing here."

"Would there be any benefit to my coming down there myself and looking around. I mean is there a chance that my dog is there, but she might not be described correctly on your roster?"

"Sir, I don't see what benefit that would serve. You are welcome to come down and look around if you want to," he replied condescendingly.

"May I give you my name and number so that you can call me if anybody reports or brings in a dog like mine?"

The volunteer takes John's name down and dutifully stated that he will call him if any calls come in that fit Chloe's description.

Friday passed and there was no sign of Chloe.

It's a sad time when you've lost a dog and a night passes. You worry if they are safe or cold. You beat yourself up because you begin to ask yourself how in the world you let this happen again. You vow to never again allow your silly dog to be without a collar.

"I am going to give all her baths with her collar on in the future. Why did I take it off in the first place? I also will not lock the front door ever again. Why haven't we done that dog-chip thing where they implant something to help you find a lost dog? Never again, never again am I going to allow this to happen to us or Chloe," John told Karen.

At first glance, Chloe looked like a well behaved thoroughbred who loved strangers. So when someone picked her up they thought they had found something "valuable." This trait in addition to her other qualities prompted her finders to instantly entertain the prospect of keeping her. This in large part complicated the problem of losing Chloe and then recovering her if she did not have her collar.

"Someone must love this dog. I can tell by how she trusts people. This dog has never been mistreated," John and Karen imagined the "finder" saying when they had Chloe in the car and then subsequently in their home.

The bad thing about Chloe's being so good was that the people who were tempted to keep her were less likely to take her to the pound. They preferred to just call thus further hampering the recovery efforts of John and Karen.

Anyway, it had been three days, it was a Saturday and no news about Chloe. Karen and John had called the pound about ten times. John makes rounds at the hospital that day and was about to come home, but for some reason decided to go to the pound and look around for himself. It seemed odd to him when he got there. He had a sense of fear and anxiety, feeling nauseated and experiencing intense butterflies. It almost felt like scenes he'd seen in movies where someone goes to the morgue to identify the body of a loved one. He began to beat himself up yet again, thinking that this will be the time they won't be getting Chloe back.

"I am John McHugh. I have lost my dog. May I look around to see if she is here?"

"What does she look like?"

John described Chloe and added things like, "She has a patch of frilly hair just behind her neck and a big bump on her back like a mole or something. She is very sweet."

The attendant looks through his roster of dogs and finds no match.

"I don't see one that looks like that."

"May I look around anyway?"

"Sure. Knock yourself out."

"How insensitive," John thought. "Knock yourself out? I am dying here and my heart is about to explode. I don't want to see all the dogs in there either waiting to be found, given away or living by a thread on death row."

The guy tells John there are two areas inside. The first area houses the new-founds, which are desirable, and your marquee thoroughbred appearing dogs. The second area houses those who have been here for over three days, not as desirable looking and close to facing euthanasia. (No, I am not referring to the children in China.)

John is directed to a side door behind the desk and enters the aisles of cages that hold the dogs. The characteristic pound smell hit him as the door opened. It is at once a familiar dog smell mixed with an antiseptic-type odor. "An institutional smell," John said to himself. He thought, "Please let her be here," remembering vividly all the times he had been to the pound before without results.

Around the aisles he went and it was a sad sight. As he walked he passed row after row of cute dogs in their little cages and he noted that the cages were all clean and each had fresh water. His sense was that the Humane Society appeared to be doing a conscientious job in terms of cleanliness and attending to the basic needs of the animals. If Chloe were there she was being cared for. All the dogs just sat there and waited contentedly for fate to determine their future. "Ignorance is indeed bliss," he thought. After viewing about fifty dogs, he came around the corner on the last aisle and saw a golden appearing dog with abbreviated facial features comfortably sitting in her cage perfectly content with her situation, the surroundings and new abode.

"Lo Lo, is that you?"

She characteristically wagged her bushy tail and her demeanor was as if John had disturbed her on some unknown mission. John couldn't believe he had found her and stood in front of the cage for some time marveling in the moment. He began to think about what must have transpired for Chloe over the last few days and her journey to be where she was now. She had left her home, roamed around somewhere probably for hours, picked up by either the pound or a caring individual who took the time to save her and get her to safety. He did not think to inquire as to the details of her recovery probably because subconsciously he did not want to ponder the thought that she had been alone without her family or the circuitous route she had taken to end up as a common unclaimed dog at the pound. The vision of all of that to John was an indictment against him for having been an irresponsible steward of Chloe. It was a place in his mind he did not want to go.

When John told the attendant that he had found his dog, he was told that there were some fees that needed to be settled. He was surprised at how much it was, but was very grateful to be paying it. "Quite the racket they got going on here," he thought to himself. They finally give Chloe to him after what felt like hours of "processing." He walked her out to his Toyota truck and called home on his cell phone.

"Karen, this is John." Then he couldn't talk. He was absolutely overcome with emotion.

"John, are you there? Is everything okay? Are you all right?"

"I...found...Chloe. I am coming home with her and will be there in about fifteen minutes." "Damn," he thought to himself. He hated it when he couldn't talk because of the fear of crying. It was a trait traced back to his grandfather on his mother's side and an un-male attribute he detested. It embarrassed him.

This particular chapter in a lose-Chloe and then a find-Chloe recovery episode represented one of the few times in which John or Karen personally went to the pound and actually found her there. They decided that trusting descriptions over phone was a flawed technique to find a dog, particularly Chloe. The thought of losing Chloe when she was at the pound all along and not their having made the obligatory rounds there was a tragic scenario for them to ponder. Of course, because dogs can't' talk, they would have never known what had happened to the Chompster.

A year or so later, Chloe was gone again. There were no phone calls reporting a dog that fit Chloe's description, no sighting in the neighborhood, nothing at Ingles, no reports at the pound. Because of past experiences with the pound, John personally went down there to "walk the aisles," and still no Chloe. John purposefully and ad nauseum gave a very accurate description of her to include that her hair was becoming a mosaic of different hues of yellow, and that some of her hair, particularly on her back in random splotches, was very stiff, almost like bristles. She had these large bumps under her skin in several places that John and Karen believed to be Mastoid tumors, but held off taking her to have them removed. They were soft and movable and in John's mind meant that they were an eyesore, but not cancer. For the purposes of this discussion, they did make for an additional way to identify her.

This episode of Chloe's disappearance was a bit different than the rest. This time there was not an issue with a mistaken identity at the pound, we covered that. The emphasis for this search and recovery mission was based on finding out about reports to the Humane Society of a dog being found, but not turned in to the pound. This represented another category of people who found a dog and how they handled it. What John and Karen learned over time was that if the person who found Chloe was a "dog person," she quickly became a part of their family, but they had the decency to report her to the pound. Their plan then would be to keep Chloe, but their conscious was clear in that they had made the effort to report her. This was the case on two other occasions in which Chloe just hung out with a family until John and Karen determined her whereabouts. An example of one such occasion was when she ended up with the guy who owned a pizza place near Ingles.

"She loves sitting on our couch and watching T.V. with us and our children love sleeping with her," he said when they arrived to pick Chloe up. The faces of his children betrayed their disappointment at Chloe's owner arrival and her subsequent departure.

Once a family found Chloe, they were reluctant to let her go. She became so quickly a part of a family that they would want to make her their pet. It was a tough situation for this type of family, torn between not wanting to let her go, but at the same time wanting to do the right thing by reporting her to the Humane Society. Why would they not just pick her up and then either call to have her taken to the pound or take her there themselves? The reason was they wanted to keep her. In a round about way they hoped that they would fail in their efforts and hence just keep Chloe. If you knew Cholonesome, you'd understand.

The reason why a person would want to keep a good older dog that they had found and obviously was loved by another family is because this type of dog is hard to come by. If you have ever had a puppy with all the chewing, accidents in the house, concerns about being hit in the street or being unsafe with children, you realize the magnitude of finding a dog like Chloe. So here comes along Chloe, a member of the family minute one and right off the bat, calm, house trained, car wise, and can hold her bladder on a trip to the beach forever...it was a no brainer.

Part of Chloe's charm was the fact that despite how old she had become, she continued to have a puppy face. Everyone, particularly the people who picked her up, thought she was a puppy mature beyond her years.

"What a cute puppy. How old is she?" they asked John and Karen time and time again at "pick-up." She was fourteen in people years for goodness sakes! Looking like a puppy despite being almost 100 in dog years was part of her "shtick." Chloe knew what she was doing.

Back to this particular Chloe lost and then Chloe found story. John visited or called the pound daily for over a week which resulted in getting two phone numbers representing someone who had called in a description of a dog that matched Chloe, but had "elected" not to bring her in. Pictures of Chloe, her description given to the manager at Ingles and to some of employees there yielded no leads. No calls or sightings of her in the area around Ingles were forthcoming. John decided to call one of the numbers.

"Hello, this John McHugh. I have lost a dog that fits the description that you called in to the Humane Society. May I come by and see if you have my dog? Her name is Chloe."

"What's she look like?" is the reply somewhat curt and indignantly.

John described her to the best of his abilities as his heart raced hoping and anticipating the lady will say that everything matches up and that he can come on over and get his dog.
"Well, I'm looking at her now playing with my kids, and she don't fit that description."
"Can I come by and just verify? I have had her for twelve years. May I ask where you live?"

"No. I don't think that's necessary. This one ain't her. I can tell you that."

"May I please come by and be sure ma'am? This has happened to me before where someone thought they did not have her but they did. She has been our dog for twelve years. It is important to my family that we find her."

"No. This ain't her. Goodbye."

Now, John began to think that Chloe has landed in a home where she is so loved and easy that her qualities have overcome the conscience of the people to do the right thing. They didn't want or intend for her to be found. They have just happened upon the perfect dog, unless of course it thunders and for some reason the collar is off, then they will be in the same fix.

"They better sure as hell take care of her is all I have to say," John thought angrily to himself as the dial tone resonated in his ear.

Of course throughout all of this every time John or Karen drove on Thompson Bridge Road they had visions of seeing a yellowish looking dog on the side of the road having been hit and left there to die. The thought of this killed them and the two cringed everyday while using that busy thoroughfare for fear that they might see that visage. A life so cherished, but then so disrespected in death, alone and unclaimed at the edge of an uncaring and indifferent thoroughfare. The thought of it was horrible to envision.

John called the second number.

"Hi, I am John McHugh. The Humane Society tells me you found a dog that fits the description of one I've lost. Would it be possible for me to come by and see if she is ours?"

At this point John had the realization of something very odd. He had been checking the register of incoming calls to the pound daily and this number came in after about ten days. Why the delay? Had Chloe been out and about by herself in the elements for over a week? Did this family at first plan to keep her and then had second thoughts about what was the right thing to do? He wondered if someone picked her up thinking she is a thoroughbred and once in the car and then several miles away determine she was not, then let her out at the nearest gas station. Gas stations he thought must be the most common drop off point for this type of dog picker-uppers. Over the years John and Karen had found Chloe several times at convenience stores over ten miles from their home and believed this was the most likely explanation of her being found so far away from home. This was a more likely scenario than that she walked the entire distance. The thought of Chloe walking alongside back roads in the cold and alone because of their negligence was a painful one for John and Karen.

The person on the phone from the get-go was much more pleasant and educated in her demeanor than the other person he had called earlier.

"Sure. Can you describe her please? We found her so cold and wet. She was very weak and hungry." (John didn't want to buy that. He thought, "Here we go again. I am sorry, but why do these dog-finders always feel like they have to throw in that guilt stuff at me. I don't know if it's to make an owner feel guilty for being a bad caretaker of their pet, or to justify their having picked up a dog, keeping it and not taking it to the pound.")

Ignoring the probable manufactured and inflated sob story about how Chloe was found, John described Chloe to the lady's satisfaction and she agrees to let him come by to verify his ownership.

"Where do you live?" he asked.

"In the subdivision just beyond McEver Road on Dawsonville Highway."

"Dawsonville Highway? Ma'am that is about fifteen miles from here. Where did you find her?"

"At the convenience store near our home," and the voice then adds yet again, but now with a whiney pathetic tone, "She was so weak and lonely. We felt obliged to bring her home. As you come into the subdivision we are the fifth house on the right, it's grey. We will be in the front yard planting some shrubs."

John asks himself, "Did I just ask that? I knew better than to subject myself to this again."

As John drove there he began to hope he would find Chloe, but more than that he wondered, "How in the world did she get all the way over there? She must have been picked up, carried a distance, let off and then found." He reasoned that someone picked her up because she looked like a golden retriever puppy and finding she was neither, let her out at the nearest convenience store. He pulled into the subdivision, again his heart pounded as he surveyed the fifth house on the right. He scanned carefully the street, yard and garage. He saw the couple working in front of their house, but he didn't see a dog milling about that looked like Chloe. He parked, got out of his car, and a very attractive couple approached.

"I am John McHugh. I called about my dog."

"Hi, John," the lady said, and then introduced herself and her husband.

All the while John continued to look around for Chloe. "Is this or is this not where Chloe ended up," he thought. He sees nothing.

"John, can you further describe your dog to us please?"

"What is this?" John began to think. "Why do all these people who find dogs feel they then have to become their protectorate from the very people trying to get their dog back? Chloe why do you do this to me? Who in the hell do they think they are? Then it dawned on him. "There must be folks out there who get the names of lost dogs from the pound and then go about to check out these dogs to claim them for their own. Maybe it is a common scheme and an easy yet inexpensive way to get lost thoroughbred dogs. He had never thought about this scenario before, but if people will steal power cords to a boat dock for the copper, they'd try to get a good dog and then sell it. John patiently decided to play along. These seemed to be very decent people who wanted to make sure that the owner and the dog matched. It was now clear and apparent; they had Chloe and they too had fallen under Chlomsome's spell.

"She has a black spot on her tongue. Her name is Chloe. She has a bushy tail. It is cut that way on purpose. We sometimes call her "Le Plume" because of how it looks. She has features like a golden retriever, but if you look at her closer she has too short a nose and her ears are way too small. Her nose and ears don't fit her head exactly the right way. My wife thinks it's the chow in her."

The lady responds, "Anything else. Any other description which you feel will definitively identify her?"

John now thought, "What is it going to take to prove to these people that this dog is mine? Being forced to jump through so many hoops to prove this is Chloe must mean they have her. Strangers love her and she loves them. Time and time again she had adopted a new family and the family immediately fell in love with her. I may have to pry her away from these people."

He realized, "They don't want to let her go without a fight."

He got it. He knew what these people were going through better than they knew themselves.

John then said, "She has a rash around her neck where the collar has rubbed off her hair. It is splotchy and slightly reddened." And then in a defensive moment added, "That is why her collar identifying her was not on when she ran away, we were letting it heal."

The lady calls to her husband and said dejectedly, "Honey, this is the owner. Go get Bear."

That the lady called Chloe "Bear" no longer surprised John. He knew exactly what had happened. They had fallen in love with her and had given Chloe "their" name. He had seen this phenomenon before. It was okay and he expected this considering it had been

about ten days in which this couple had been exposed to
Chlonely.

John's heart was no longer beating fast. After this telling
interrogation there was no doubt he had found Chloe. It was only
a matter of time now. Out of the shadows of their garage ambled
a dog, with a bit of limp, light in color, but shorter than a golden.
Before coming over to John, she veered to the right to some
shrubs and went to the bathroom (a marking my spot type
maneuver more than really having to go), scooted dirt in Chloe's
characteristic fashion alternating a front paw with the opposite
back paw spraying dirt and grass, and then casually sniffing a
neighbor's dog that was near the property line marked by shrubs.
Showing off, she rolled over, wriggled to scratch her back and in
the process made a "Chloe angel" in the compressed grass, and
then righted herself.

As an afterthought she recognized John's white van and slowly waddled over to him. It made John feel great to see her and he could not believe he'd found her again, forgiving the snub of her belated approach and their reunion. It was clear the couple had taken very good care of Chloe, had loved her, and were "dog people." Chloe looked great.

"Combo, we've missed you. How are you doing girl? Let's go home you big old Chlomps?"

John opened up the passenger side of the van and without hesitation or fanfare Chloe hopped up in the seat as if she were a person, as usual.

John looked at the couple and said, "Thanks so much for taking such good care of her. We are very grateful to you."

"She is a wonderful dog. We will miss sleeping with her at night. She is so well behaved and kind. Our daughter is visiting next week from Denver and we had planned to give Bear, I mean Chloe, to her to take back if we did not find the owner. We are glad we put you two back together."

"I can't wait to call my wife and family. They won't believe it. This is amazing. I would like to do something for you."

In unison the couple said, "That won't be necessary."
"Have ya'll ever eaten at our Country Club in Gainesville?"

"No we are actually new to the area."

"My wife and I would like ya'll to be our guest there one night. You'll enjoy the view of the lake and hopefully a nice meal. If you will give me your names, I can tell a friend of mine who works there to expect you. This would be the least my family could do for you in return for your kindness. Chloe insists," John said as Chloe looked on approvingly from the front seat of the van.

John did not expect them to take him up on their offer, but they did. About three weeks later he received a thank-you note from the couple telling John and Karen how much they enjoyed their evening out. The note ended with, "I hope Chloe is doing well. Tell her we said hello and thanks for dinner."

Chapter Five-The perfect escape

This time was different. Chloe had been missing for two weeks and there was nothing encouraging upon inquiring at the call-in register at the Humane Society. John and Karen were told that after one week it would be doubtful that there would be a pick-up or bring-in at that point and rarer still after two weeks. It seemed that their "finding Chloe luck" had run its course. It dawned upon them that she had had more than her obligatory "nine lives." They felt she was either happily thriving in another home and in another family's life, or she was dead. Karen made sporadic calls to the Humane Society during those two weeks, continued with notices at Ingles and on the neighborhood power poles, but after a month, for the most part, she and John gave up. Every time they passed a carcass on the busy road near their home there followed the now familiar nauseating close inspection to be sure it was not Chloe. In their hearts, they believed she was okay because someone always found her, but doubt existed. As hope of Chloe returning was reluctantly relinquished, they prayed she was safe and with someone who loved her.

"That is how it always happened with Chloe, wasn't it? She is with someone. They are in love with her about now, we know it," they reasoned.

It was now December and the prevailing optimistic view that she was safe somewhere else made the whole affair easier to bear. It was comforting to believe that she was warm somewhere in someone's house, on a couch watching T.V. with the new loving family who were in turn counting their blessings for having found her and having her in their life. Visions of happy children in bed with her on her back and having her belly rubbed helped John and Karen cope. They were okay with it. They had had their blessed time with her. They had a sense that she was part of a bigger plan.

By December she had been missing about three months and from a mental aspect the couple officially gave up in terms of actively doing things to find or recover her. As it happened, Karen bought a puppy for one of their children as a surprise, but it was not workable for him to have a puppy in the winter and living in an apartment. So John and Karen kept the dog, a chocolate lab, and she was named Penelope by the son who could not keep her at that time.

All of the unrequited love pent up inside the couple to lavish upon the triumphant return of Chloe was now heaped upon the new puppy Penelope. They fell in love with her head over heal and with a vengeance. Memories of Chloe, though cherished, slowly became less intense with time and were archived to that remote happy portion of a person's mind struggling reluctantly to move on with life.

Chapter Six-The dilemma

t had been about three months since Chloe's final disappearance and Christmas time was upon Gainesville, Georgia. John was on his way home from work one evening and happened to see what appeared to be a nativity scene in front of the First Baptist Church. He could tell that something different was happening on the expansive grounds in front of the city's largest church. There were more lights than usual and more activity than a routine nativity scene. He decided to detour from his normal route home and check it out.

What he saw was a nativity scene dramatically highlighted by lights. The church's leadership months before had decided to have a live nativity scene with all the attendant participants and accoutrements. An attempt to emphasize the "reason for the season" was the expressed purpose and it looked to him that no expense was spared to make the scene historically authentic. John saw numerous farm type vehicles to the side of the church to support the needs of all the animals being used. When he arrived it was just about dark and all the elements of the nativity scene were getting into their respective places. Between the characters who were dressed in their costumes and the people helping organize the production, John estimated about fifty or so people were involved with the project and it was clear the church had made a large financial and time commitment to its success. In the sky behind the scene was a perfect rendition of the Star of Bethlehem. On closer inspection the star, suspended just above the nativity scene, appeared very real and had been formed by a laser apparatus. The star in addition to the live animals made the nativity scene look real and very professional.

"I can't wait to tell Karen about this. She'll love seeing it. It looks like the Baptist Church has one-upped the Methodists on this one. Our plywood "un-live" nativity scene with one spot light to illuminate it will never do after they see this," John thought as he watched the nativity scene materialize. In a matter of minutes a perfect nativity scene appeared as if an apparition. Just as the sun had set and darkness prevailed, the nativity scene became at once isolated and illuminated. The lights for the church were gone, the cars and farm vehicles faded into darkness and only the participants remained. It was something to see. The cast of animals, people in character, the lights, the manger and the star in their totality was not only beautiful, it was moving.

"I think they have pulled something off here. This is good. I don't know what it cost, but if they wanted to make people to stop, look, and then think about the birth of Christ, they've done it," he thought.

John tried to remember who and what should actually be in a nativity scene. Whenever he saw a nativity scene, he thought about the definition of "manger." For a large part of his life he thought that the manger was the same thing as a nativity scene. It was only recently he learned the manger is the feeding trough Jesus was laid in and only a small, though significant, part of the nativity scene.

"I bet most people think the manger is the same thing as the nativity scene too," he thought. "If I've thought that I bet others have," he reasoned to himself. What he saw unfolding before him made him ponder Christmas in general and the nativity scene in particular. The activities and scene took on almost a carnival atmosphere, but without the large canvas "big top" or gaudiness. The intentions of the church's leadership, in John's mind, had reached its full fruition.

"Let's see, there should be the star of Bethlehem, Mary and Joseph, Baby Jesus in the manger, some sheep, some shepherds, some farm animals like cows and donkeys, the three kings with their camels, and lots of hay strewn about," he said to himself as he began to critique the scene before him. As a mental exercise he wanted to verify the historical and biblical correctness of what he was witnessing.

And then he saw something! He could not believe his eyes. He sees it just as he is leaving to tell Karen how moving his experience had been. John said to himself, "What if I had left and not seen this?"

John looked on in amazement as the crowd of onlookers slowly increased in number and the nativity scene took its final and most perfect and symmetrical form. In addition to the biblical characters and animals, John noticed a small boy cradling what at first appears to be a baby lamb. Their presence nicely filled out the nativity on one hand but was a bit awkward on the other. John did not remember a small boy as being part of the biblical story. This portion of what was before John intrigued him and he peered closer. The baby lamb in the child's lap was in actuality a dog disguised with lamb's ears. Someone had even placed a jacket on the dog that looked like lamb's wool. Something about that lamb, or rather dog, was familiar. What was it? It was not so much the physical appearance as much as its countenance. It was lying there next to the child motionless, perfectly content to be dressed up as a lamb. The child seemed equally as content. It was clear they were very comfortable, not only in this manufactured situation, but with each other as well. The dog belonged to the child, and the dog was obviously very special.

John moved further through the crowd to get a closer look. His premonition was correct the dog was Chloe. He had not seen her for three months, but her characteristic features, which he and his family loved so much and knew so well, were unmistakable. She had much more hair than Karen would have allowed but her bushy tail was intact. Karen had preferred frequent hair cuts to accentuate the signature nature of Chloe's tail. When Chloe got haircuts, Brenda at "The Animal House" did not put her in a cage before or after her haircut. She let her roam around in the cutting area as if Chloe were her pet, an example to all of the other dog customers of "appropriate behavior."

"She is such a well behaved and gentle dog. She loves getting her haircut. I love just having her around," Brenda would tell Karen.

Maybe that is why Karen got Chloe's haircut so often, as therapy for the haircutter.

Chloe's chin was resting on the child's lap and she stayed perfectly still in keeping with the live manger scene. The pudgy nose, the short ears, the multi-hued hair and her demeanor confirmed the dog as being Chloe.

"What should I do? I can't get her now. Maybe I should wait until the manger scene is over and claim her then. Who is this boy she is with? Could this be who Chloe is living with now? Wonder who this child's parents are and if they are here? I am not just going to go up to the child and take Chloe. I may need to find out who his parents are and make known to them that she is my dog and I want her back. We would probably need to "arrange" a pick-up after a period of time so that the parents can prepare this boy for Chloe's departure," John thought as the complexity of recovering Chloe became more apparent to him.

John decides that it would not be the best thing to do to take Chloe from the child at this juncture. No, he couldn't do that. He reasons that he would need to find out who the parents were and speak with them. He already was anticipating the now very familiar interrogation that would follow his claiming that Chloe was his dog. It would not be a pretty situation particularly since it was clear the boy and Chloe had become such comfortable companions.

"How long will this nativity scene be going on?" he asked another on looker.

"Tomorrow night is the last night," he was told.

"Who is that little boy with lamb, I mean dog? That is something else, I mean how they are sitting there so peacefully and for such a long time," John asked.

"I don't know. I was just saying the same thing to my wife. We both had noticed how the two of them are at peace with each other. They are stealing the show all right. Look at that dog, he hasn't moved from that boy's lap for almost an hour now. My dog won't let you put anything on him much less an entire lamb's outfit. The lights alone would spook my dog," the man said. He then added, "You think that dog is a puppy. That makes this all the more fascinating."

John smiled, "No, I bet she's not a puppy. I can see white hair around her eyes and mouth. That probably means she's older."

"Sure looks like a puppy to me," the man said.

John's first reaction is to rush through the crowd and hug Chloe feeling that finding his dog outweighed any disruption of the nativity scene, but he thought better of it. He decided to go home and speak to Karen about it. This was not going to be as easy as just showing up and retrieving Chloe. Getting her "the right way" would require a plan and must be done tactfully. Yes, he needed Karen's input on this.

John verifies the time of the nativity scene for the next night and excitedly went home with the knowledge he had found Chloe in, of all places, a nativity scene dressed up as a lamb.

Chapter Seven-Chloe's plan revealed

John finds Karen in the kitchen.

"Karen, I have the most amazing thing to tell you. I think I have found Chloe!"

"What? You're kidding. Where?"

John could not wait to tell the details. It was so Chloe.

"She is playing the role of a lamb in the First Baptist Church's live nativity scene. She actually looks pretty good as a lamb. She's got little lamb's ears, a fluffy wool outfit, and everything. Actually the lamb's ears don't look much different than her own."

"This is a joke, right?"

"No. I saw the lights from a nativity scene on the front lawn of the First Baptist Church on my way home and decided to go look at it. They have made a big deal of it. It looks like a movie set complete with animals, lighting and even a laser show for the Star of Bethlehem. It is something else."

"How do you know it's Chloe, John?"

"How would I not know, Karen? Duh! Her nose, those ears and the fact that she is sitting in a little boy's lap and did not move the whole time I was there. She was the star of the show, I'm telling you."

"Why don't you have her? Where is she? Is she with you?"

"I guess she is with the little boy and his family. I left before it was over. The last reenactment is tomorrow evening. I thought we might arrange to get her then. I first wanted a chance to talk things over with you. I did not want to just go up and take her from the nativity scene. I mean the boy obviously loves her and she had on that whole precious lamb's costume. It would not have been right. There were also about fifty people there looking at this thing and they would have all seen the spectacle of my recovering Chloe."

"So you find Chloe and then you just leave her there? John what in the world were you thinking?"

"What would you have done Karen? Think about it. The more I thought about it the more difficult a situation than I first realized. Do you want to be the one that goes up and claims her? You need to see this little boy and how Chloe dotes on him. We need to put our heads together on this one and think it through."

Karen stood there shaking her head in disbelieve at the thought of finding Chloe after all this time and began to consider the prospect of getting her back. As she considered what John had said, she too acknowledged to herself that this was going to be a tricky situation.

"Did you get the boy's name? Do you know who his parents are?"

"I asked one guy, but he did not know. He and his wife were quite taken by Chloe's stage presence. He asked me if I thought Chloe was a puppy. Is that funny or what? How many times have we been asked that?"

"At least we know where she is, that she is all right and being loved. That alone means a lot to me. I have just now stopped having nightmares about her being hit by a car, left on the side of the road and then riding by and seeing it. So this is good news. Now, what to do?" said Karen.

"Exactly," John said now feeling that Karen understood the gravity as well as the complexity of their dilemma. Chloe was always doing this type of thing to them, they were used to it.
John then asked, "What would you do and how would you feel if after having Chloe for three months the true owner showed up to claim her? Maybe that is the way we should view this now."

"This is different John. We have lived and breathed Chloe for fourteen years. We have practically raised our children around her. Think of what we have been through with her. The lost and found episodes alone I think justify getting her back. We owe it to Chloe don't you think?"

"I just keep seeing the little boy's face in that scene and how it will look and how he'll feel if we were to go and take Chloe from him."

Karen responded, "It will be difficult John, but when I think about what is right and fair, getting back a dog we've had for so long is a reasonable thing to do. I don't see how anyone would fault us for that. This may sound odd to you, but I think it's important for her to be buried next to Meg in the woods above our front yard."

This back and forth reasoning went on for hours. One moment Karen was the proponent of getting Chloe back and then the next that the little boy should keep her. The same thing happened with John as the two played out all the scenarios they could think of. They even consider a compromise of either joint custody or bargaining for visitation rights. They did agree on one thing. They would not tell their children, who were all out of the house (but not out of mind) and older, about sighting Chloe. They decide not to ask for their input, they knew what they'd say and that would only complicate matters.

The two gravitate to a solution which John commonly used to deal with difficult decisions both personal and professionally. They agree to do nothing, for now.

"Let's get more information Karen before we make a decision. What if she is now in a really nice home and is very happy? Look at it this way, we still have Penelope."

Karen says, "Well I guess we could go to the nativity and get a feel for things. It might be she is so happy that we'll easily agree to leave her with her present family. We could follow the boy and his family home and see if it is a good situation. I do not want her living on a busy street or an area that is not safe to run around in and play. You know how much she enjoys chasing squirrels. This prompted a smile and prompts a nice memory of Chloe. Chloe loved to stalk and then chase squirrels. John had videoed at least fifty unfruitful attempts by Chloe to catch a squirrel. She was never close, but she never gave up. As she aged and arthritis kicked in, the attempts became comical. She'd chase a squirrel that easily got away and Karen would remark, "Good girl Chloe, you almost got that one!" Karen rewarded her for the failed effort while patting and rubbing her fur. She didn't want to hurt Chloe's feelings. Karen knew how important it was to Chloe to be a legitimate squirrel chaser.

After discussing everything they could think of, they reached a consensus. They would go to the Baptist church the next evening to size up the situation, follow the family home, consider what they had gleaned and then make a decision. It had been at least three months since they had seen Chloe; it was not as if they had to be in a hurry about it.

The next morning Karen awoke to a new found realization and change in heart. She now felt Chloe was within their grasp and it was right and proper to tell the new family Chloe was their dog. It could be done in a civil and gentle way if both parties were clever about it. John on the other hand was still conflicted, waiting for the tincture of time and thought to deliver the answer that felt good to him. John had seen the scene at the church with the boy, Karen had not. Karen considered this and then resigned herself to withholding judgment until that evening. Both awaited the time apprehensively. Thinking about having to confront the boy and his family regarding Chloe's true owners sent waves of butterflies across their chests throughout that day.

Karen and John arrive at the church at about the time the laser fired up and as the support crews and vehicles made their exit. The sight was more magnificent than the night before. The reality of the nativity scene was the thing that was so impressive. Large farm animals each emanated a foggy mist from of their nostrils as they breathed the characteristic chilly air of a southern December night. The cast of characters, all so adroitly dressed in such time dated and beautiful costumes, completed the scene.

Karen feverishly made her way through the crowd in anticipation of seeing Chloe. She had in her mind the possibility that the dog John saw may not have been Chloe, that he may have been mistaken. She panned the whole scene and spotted the little boy dressed as a Shepherd's son and a dog.

"John, you are right. That's Chloe. No doubt about it. It really isn't about how she looks. It's because she is so at peace. She's up there like a queen holding court. I have missed her so. I am tempted to go up there right now and love on her like we used to," she said rhetorically since she and John had already agreed to watch the entire event, check out the family's home situation and then later discuss their next step.

The little boy, who Karen guessed to be about eight, and Chloe stole the show. The animals in their immenseness in addition to the other participants by virtue of their sheer number were impressive, but the boy and the dog dressed as a lamb sitting perfectly still and lovingly embraced, glaringly stood out. John and Karen sensed others felt the same way because they overheard people comment on the little boy, how well he was acting and how proud of him they were. The child seemed to be someone who all the members of the church knew by sight. It also seemed they took a bit more interest in the child than just any child. John and Karen's thoughts however did not dwell there; they were thinking ahead to the detective like plan they had concocted to determine the suitability of Chloe's new home.

John said, as they were looking on, "How far back do we stay in the car so they won't know we're following them? I mean, don't we need a technique or a strategy for this. How do they do it in the movies? "

Karen makes a face, the "John is being inappropriate again" face and continued to dissect the scene before her. Two things intrigued her. Who were this child's parents? She surveyed the area about the manger for anyone who looked like a significant other and did not see anyone that might be the parent of the boy. The second thing was the boy himself. How was it that a child this age stayed so well behaved and seated throughout this whole production? She understood about Chloe doing it, but a young child? She thought of her children, "They would be knocking over the manger about now and pulling somebody's hair."

The roped off area limiting how close to the nativity scene spectators could stand was further away from the manger than usual because of the livestock. The concern about the risk of someone being injured by an erratic movement of one of the animals had probably prompted this precaution. Because of this John and Karen were standing about a hundred feet from where the boy and Chloe were sitting. After about an hour and with the temperature dropping, a church official walked out in front of the nativity scene marking its end. He made a short speech thanking all the participants and the people who had helped with the animals, costumes, and the necessary logistics associated with such an ambitious project. The First Baptist Church edifice, which had been a second cousin and an unlighted backdrop to the nativity scene, now became illuminated showing the large Greek columns that framed it. At the same time all of the ancillary lights for the nativity scene, including the Star of Bethlehem, vanished. The animals and other participants milled around in the shadows of the church that had reasserted its rightful place as the primary object of interest on the property.

"We need to keep our eye on them John. If we don't, we will lose Chloe again. Chloe's bad that way," Karen said as she and John slowly crept in toward the manger scene. The support crew moved in to began the dissimulation of props and the herding of the animals to their respective transportation vehicles.

Chloe and the little boy remained seated. This stood out to both John and Karen and was somewhat out of place in light of the anxious and hurried movement all about the boy and Chloe. The scene had the look of a computer-generated swirl with a focused picture in the center surrounded by a blurred circular frame. John and Karen continued to move carefully toward the boy and Chloe. Instinctively, they both looked around as if they were being watched or that their intentions might be detected. They then did something they rarely did in public, their hands clasped. It happened unintentionally and when it did John and Karen's eyes met for a second as they continued on their mission.

John thought at that instant, "Why is it that something dramatic has to happen with my family to realize how much I love Karen? I need to act and feel this way all the time even when things are going perfectly. Wives and prayer are similar that way."

"A person's faith unfortunately is a lot like that too," he reflected.

The two stopped at the same moment about thirty feet from the boy and Chloe. They now had the same thought. Chloe had been their family's dog for fourteen years and there was no reason to feel guilty about claiming her. They had a history with this dog, the new people no matter how cute the boy, did not. Though not spoken, they mutually had made their decision. It was apparent in how the two looked at each other and in the tension they felt in each other's hand, "We want our Chloe back and we want her now." They walked with renewed resolve toward the now dimly lit nativity scene and the still seated boy and Chloe.

With an intestinal fortitude that surprised themselves, they marched toward Chloe to reclaim what they now felt emphatically was rightfully theirs. Their minds were made up. And then it happened. It was as if it occurred in super slow motion. When Karen was ten feet away and about to claim Chloe, a woman appeared, entered the space occupied by the boy and Chloe and began speaking to them. She was obviously the boy's mother.

"Stop John, stop!" said Karen.

"What? What are you talking about?" asked John.

"Just stop. Let's stand here for a minute and watch. This may be the boy's mother. Look at Chloe and how she is looking at the boy and his mother. No father? Where is the boy's father? I bet she is a single mother John. Oh my word, this is getting very complicated. Stop walking, let's just watch."

Seeing the mother caused Karen and John to consider reverting back to the original plan. They would observe, take mental notes, follow them home, assess the situation and then make a decision about how aggressively to reclaim the Chlompster-miester supremo, if at all. But that plan changed yet again as Karen saw Chloe's features and her familiar persona, as they drew closer to her.

"John, I've changed my mind. I am telling them that Chloe is ours. John, she is our dog. She has been an integral part of our family for so many years. We have a history. She's the same dog I hit with my car and then nursed to health. We nursed her through the broken shoulder when she fell off our porch. She has slept in our bedroom for over fourteen years John; you just don't let that go. She is our Chloe. Let's get her and take her home where she belongs. Can you imagine how the children will feel when we tell them we have found Chloe, or how they would feel if we had found her but let her go? I think we should tell these people she is ours. I am sorry John but, she is our dog and we love her too."

Around the boy and Chloe, several people were shaking the mother's hand and patting her on the back in what appeared to be a congratulatory fashion. It soon became clear to John and Karen that she was being complimented for her son's performance. She made a loving facial expression to the boy and Chloe as she made her way closer to them after speaking with the well-wishers.

Just as John and Karen were preparing to assert their ownership, the woman positions herself to the side of the boy, bended over and picked him up and started to walk away toward a van. The boy's legs were lifeless and dangled helplessly draped over his mother's arms. His eyes, head and upper body were animated, but his lower extremities only swayed in lockstep with the mother's gait. As the women carried the boy to the van, its side door opened and a wheelchair enabled lift descended in anticipation of its passenger. The child was placed in his wheelchair which in turn was lifted into the van. As the van door for the wheelchair closed, the mother in a fluid motion opened the passenger door and Chloe hopped in. John and Karen witnessed the events unfolding before them in awe and disbelief.

"What had they almost done?" they thought. Whatever internal pledge they had made to claim Chloe was now shattered. The mother got into the van, started the engine, and began to leave the church parking lot.

As the van was leaving, John and Karen continued to watch its departure and remained speechless as they drifted together, hand in hand, to the curb of the parking lot where the van had just been. Surprisingly, the van stopped short of the parking lot exit, backed up, and then returned to where John and Karen were standing. The woman pulled the van alongside the curb and rolled down the passenger side window. In doing so she unknowingly placed Chloe inches away from her previous life and family. John and Karen were at a loss of what to do and were confused as to why the lady had come back to the very point where they were standing. Did she suspect something? Did Chloe do something to prompt the lady's return?

"Excuse me," she said. "Do you by chance see a collar on the ground near this area? Our dog has the worst habit of losing it."

John and Karen look down and exactly half way between them was Chloe's collar.

Karen, as she stooped to pick up the collar said, "Here it is."

John looked at Chloe closely. Same old ears, same old pudgy nose, same old happy puppy face, and same old wagging bushy tail making a swishing sound on the car seat. "If I had a penny for every time she rode with me in that 86 Toyota truck, I'd be a rich man," John thought. Sizing his dog up he thought, "Chloe's playing it cool. She knows who we are. Two can play this game my old friend," as he looked intently into her mature white hair encircled brown eyes.

"How old is your puppy?" John asked with a smile.

"She's not a puppy, but I don't really know how old she is. She must be pretty old because she has a little limp from arthritis. We have had her only three months. She just showed up one day at our house. She has truly been a blessing to my son. They are best friends."

As Karen was handing the collar to the lady, she glanced at the nametag.

"Her name is Sam? That's an interesting name for a girl dog."

As the lady gently and lovingly placed the collar on Chloe's neck she said, "Her real name is Samantha, but we call her Sam. In the Old Testament Sam means *from God* and that is exactly what she is to us, a gift from God. You cannot imagine how much she has meant to my son and the confidence she gives him. There is no way he would have been in this nativity scene without her. He is a changed person and our family is so blessed because of her."

John said, "Have you ever considered getting one of those chip things implanted. They'd come in handy if she were to lose her collar and then you lost her."

John and Karen petted Chloe through the van's window for what they now knew would be the last time. The lady began petting Chloe as well. At that moment out the darkness from the rear of the van a little boy's hand appeared and also began stroking Chloe. At that moment, four different hands connected to four different hearts were all caressing Chloe in unison, but yet each feeling the same love and emotion for her.

Then the mother said, "Come on Sam, let's all go home and watch *It's a Wonderful Life*. Thank ya'll for finding Sam's collar and I think I'll take you up on the suggestion about getting a chip implanted."

As the passenger side window moved up, Chloe's face faded behind the reflection of John and Karen's silhouette in the glass. The glare from the now lighted church made it difficult to see Chloe's features and she slowly disappeared as the window closed. The van slowly edged away and departed the parking lot, leaving John and Karen alone to ponder Chloe.

"Merry Christmas Chloe," they whispered together as the van disappeared and they relinquished their beloved dog to the little boy and his new family.
"John?"

"Yes."

"Chloe may lose her collar again, but she'll never be lost."

"How so?" asked John.

"I think Chloe has finally been found by the family she was looking for."

And then as an afterthought and with a reflective smile Karen said, "Sam, huh? Hebrew for, *from God*. How fitting."

After several minutes and the van no longer in sight, John said, "Karen, let's get home to Penelope. I call dibs on giving her a chicken treat."

Lost Dog

Lost dog, that's what the sign said
When she hung it on the telephone pole

Lost dog, I hope she finds him
And I hope he finds his way home

He wouldn't sit, He wouldn't beg
He was bad and he would not play ball

She couldn't do anything with him
But without him she was nothing at all

Lost dog, that's what the sign said
When she hung it on the telephone pole

Lost dog, I hope she finds him
And I hope he finds his way home

He was a thief, he stole her heart
He was a rambler, a rogue and a rook

He wouldn't come when she called him
And she called him every name in the book

Lost dog, that's what the sign said
When she hung it on the telephone pole

Lost dog, I hope she finds him
And I hope he finds his way back home

Rusty McHugh

Epilogue

Okay I made up the last chapter. I have never written fiction before and must say I enjoyed taking a stab at it. The mother coming back for Chloe's collar at the end was clever I thought. Here's what really happen to the Chlomiester, the real last chapter of her most beautiful life.

I bet this has never happened to you. One of our sons wanted a chocolate lab so my wife took it on as a life mission to get one. She looks at several and then goes to see one in Buford, Ga.

"When she saw me she came right to me. I knew she was the one," Karen says when she comes home with the new puppy.

She was pretty, but all I could see was the trouble of training a puppy and all which that entailed. You know the accidents in the house and the like. Then after further consideration the son decided that because he lived in an apartment and his place was on the third floor it was decided that raising a puppy would not be ideal in this situation. Presto- chango we have a new dog. I must say the color chocolate is indeed the most beautiful of colors on a dog. We had never had a lab before and for that matter a chocolate dog; they are hard to see at night. Shortly after getting her my wife takes a trip and for the first time I am in complete charge of Penelope. She had a crate that we were in hopes of using just like they say in all the books and in the way all of our silly friends use the crate.

"Oh the crate is wonderful. Our dog loves it and will stay in it happily while we are at work," they say.

Well the crate has never worked for us and I have several of various sizes and designs in the garage covered with spider webs to prove it. (Just like all the lampshades from vet visits.)

Karen is gone and I come home from work to find Penelope in the crate and she and all of the blankets and toys in the crate are covered with excreta. I mean the stuff is all in her paws and on all the wires of the crate. This is like having a baby, do you remember? When a child is just home from the hospital it is a bit strange. I mean you don't love it immediately, how could you? You just met. So at this point I don't have a relationship with Penelope and this as the first thing coming home from work and my wife gone for three days just "did not suit" as my mother used to say. The first night that my wife was gone I get up at the time we have been taking her out, about 2 a.m., and walk outside with her. It was full moon and as I was going out I see a possum slowly walking across the front yard as if in a trance. It was the damnedest thing; I had only seen them playing dead in our trash cans or as road kill. I decide to let Penelope just roam to use the bathroom and at that moment she takes off into the woods. Gone. Because she is chocolate I can't see her. Forty five minutes of calling, looking for motion or sound and my heart racing as I am thinking, "If anything happens to this dog I am toast with Karen." I go to road thinking I need to clear that area first and nothing. Undecided whether to go up the road or down to search a larger perimeter I go down. Then as by chance in a group of Leyland Cypresses I see movement of a branch and there she is. It is like when someone hides something from you as a prank and you finally find it you are torn between being angry versus you now have something you thought you lost and relief in finding it. My emotions registered with the latter and never again would she be "off lease" if it were dark.

It was a funny thing, with all our other dogs we just let them out and then let them in when they wanted (An indoor outdoor dog). We had no fences and never had a dog, other than our first dog Fancy, hit by a car. But all sorts of things started changing with Penelope, this was the first dog picked out exclusively by Karen. Oh yes, soon we started getting chicken strips to give out as treats. We'd never done that before. Karen was treating Penelope as she was special. Then I come home one day and the back yard is completely fenced in complete with a gate leading off the back porch. We had lived in this house for fifteen years for heaven's sake. Meg nor Chloe ever got chicken treats and they did not need a gate. The two dachshunds never needed a gate. Tootsie the little girl dachshund would stay unattended for a week if we went to the beach. She'd hover around the garage and protect Mr. Kitten who by the way didn't need anything from anybody. So all those two needed was a neighbor to stop by once a day to re up the food and water.

Penelope and Chloe got along swimmingly and became very good playmates.

One day in particular I was out at our little cabin on Lake Lanier with the two of them, it was January. At that time I was into building fly rods from kits I'd get from Cabelas. I remember as if it were yesterday, I get a call from Karen.

"John have you seen the snow?" she asked.

I had been so intent on the fly rod building process I had not noticed. I look out and I see the most beautiful snow I have ever seen. What was unique for here in Georgia was that the flakes were huge. (Later in the week I had several older patients tell me they had never in their life time seen such large snowflakes.) It was truly very beautiful to see. Then I notice Chloe and Penelope playing in the snow. I don't mean snow on the ground but what is in the air falling. They were truly excited by it. I believe that with that snow they sealed their friendship as I had never seen them play together so fervently. Running together, biting at each other, stopping and starring each other down and then repeated the process over and over. They had a ball, and to think I could have missed it had Karen not called. I got my good camera and took a bunch of pictures and I must say they turned out pretty good.

Look at Penelope's eyes. She is chasing Chloe and snipping at her and Chloe responds in kind. Chloe looks ferocious but there is not a mean bone in her body.

Well about this time my daughter Bess comes home from her "Drops of Jupiter" (Did you think of me while you tried to find yourself out there?) experience out in Jackson Hole. She had been a waitress, a picture gallery curator, bartender, a river rafting worker, and a phlebotomist all in between skiing in the winter and camping trips on the Snake River in the summer. She had come home to do the preliminary course work to get into a nurse master's program with the Medical College of Georgia. This took about six months and while she was living with us she and her mother, again without my knowledge or blessings, go out and get a rescue border collie mix. They named him Brother. Once again we go through the bathroom accidents, attempting to use a crate and all the stuff you do to integrate a new dog into the family. I must say that Brother from the get go absolutely loved Chloe and Penelope and they all got along very well. We added Brother to the lake and river excursions that I did in the little red 1986 Toyota truck every Thursday afternoon and the weekends.

Chloe became the senior member of the group as Penelope and Brother were much more active in their playing. Chloe preferred to dabble around in the periphery of the action. Chloe was never a stick chaser, but Brother and Penelope loved it. In fact it was very frustrating to Penelope that Brother would wait on the shore

of the river or lake and then attack her as she returned with the
stick and attempt to take it.

Okay I am getting there. I am slowly developing another type of
disappearing act that Chloe did but this time with an accomplice,
our son Sam who was in school at S.C.A.D. in Savannah.

Sam needed my help moving to a new apartment in Savannah, so
Chloe and I go down in my 96 Chrysler van to assist in the moving
and bring excess furniture back. I should have never fallen for it.
Once Chloe was exposed to the smells of all those old parks in
Savannah and Sam noted the attention the girls gave her and by
extension him a plot began to materialize. Since Sam was to be
living by himself, it was a natural fit for Chloe to move to
Savannah. So when Chloe and Penelope became close friends, my

wife and I fell in love with the lab as well, and that's when my son strategically asked, "Can Chloe come to visit me in Savannah? She can stay with me until I come home for my birthday." That was about the last we saw of the Chlomiester for months. "She loves long walks on the beach at Hilton Head", he tells us. "Girls love her", he tells us. "Chloe is killing it here," he tells us. "She loves Forsyth Park," he tells us. Meanwhile all of our attention is now directed at the Pompie and we weren't sure if we'd ever get Chloe back or for that matter, if Chloe would ever want to come back. So...all the stuff we were doing with Chloe we started doing with Peppi; a Chloe clone so to speak.

Well Sam finishes S.C.A.D. after several months Miss Chloe comes home. The following is a song that Sam wrote and I had listened to it several times before I got the message of what it expresses. I mean Savannah and all those historic smells are something but Gainesville with the Lake and the River and trips in the little red truck must have rated more than it appeared on the surface. I really did not think of what I am about to say until I was writing this. What if we hurt Chloe's feelings by letting her go to Savannah with Sam? Could she have perceived this as we did not love her? Surely not, as it has been stated, she was indeed complex.

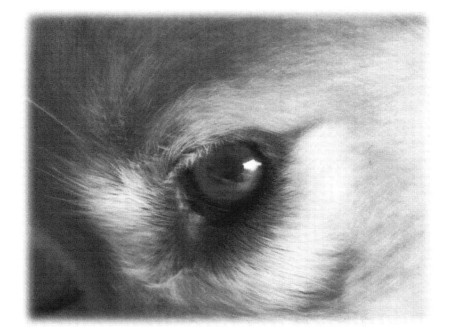

Chloe's Eyes

you're gunna find her in a field
probably over by a lake
sniffing underneath a bush
life could never be so straight

now she's in the city streets
what i call my city girl
panting in this low country heat
before we leave she starts to twirl

chloe's eyes
they don't tell
what is wrong
but she know she ain't home

yes she meets me right outside
shakes it off at the front door
making sure the coast is clear
before she sleeps on my tile floor

we're using hands as pillows now
we throw it right back on the shelf
she wouldn't use us anyway
if we tried to give our help

chloe's eyes
they don't tell
what is wrong
but she know she ain't home

So Chloe returns home after her coastal hiatus and picks up right where she left off hanging out with Penelope, who is now a regular sized dog, and Brother. Well there was one incident the weekend after Chloe got back from the low country. I had taken the three dongs to the lake and went inside the cabin to get something and when I came out there was no Chloe. Reminiscent of old times I begin to look everywhere. In the house in the bedroom, behind the cabin and the cove over there, our boat dock, the property next door and no Chloe. It was now getting dark so I get the other two dogs in the truck and slowly go up the gravel drive to the cabin and then the road that leads to cabin. At the end of this street and where the street joins an intersection I see up on hill in front of a house that is on this corner, Chloe. Just sitting and looking around. Was she looking for Sam? Had we confused her and now she wants the compact intense historic smells of Savannah? I pull up to the edge of the house's grass and open the passenger door and say, "Let's go Chlompie." She casually looks at me and ambles down the hill and gets into the truck. What is the world is in this dog's head? She had been to the lake cabin a thousand times and yet this time wanders off a half a mile to just sit and watch from a vantage point. She is indeed complex. Funny thing, she never did anything odd again like this or wandered off at the lake after having arrived back from Savannah.

Chloe had been home for about a year and Karen noticed that Chloe's abdomen seemed bigger and that her appetite was less. She took her to the vet and they gave her the option of doing a bunch of tests to see if something was going on or taking a watch and see approach. She chose the latter however after about two weeks things were getting worse not better. Chloe's mid-section was bigger and she was not eating as well but she looked happy enough and she was not in any pain. Remember in the story where her face always looked like a puppy, well her face looked great and as youthful as ever. Karen decided to have her seen by the vet again this time for definitive tests. It was a late start morning for me at work and it was a cool morning and I decided to fire up the Mustang and take Chloe to the vet on the way to work.

Karen would then check up on her and then pick her up later in the day. Chloe got in the car a nice as you please and to me she looked as good as I had ever seen her, her spirits were up and I think she looked forward to riding in the convertible as much as I did. I always try to play 60's music in the 1966 Mustang and this morning was no exception.

"This one is for you Chlompie, *Good Vibrations* by the Beach Boys Brian Wilson's masterpiece," I say. I talked to Chloe all the time.

As I recall I did not make much of this trip to the vet only that it would be fun. I knew Chloe was old now, about 15 years in human terms, but she looked good. I felt this was a bump in the road, a virus or something, and she'd back to her old self doing the stuff we always do. The pictures that follow were from the morning I took her to the vet. The sunglasses motif is because Sam's band at the time was called Sunglasses which featured Chloe's picture on the album cover and referenced her in several songs.

I had the best time taking her to the vet that morning. The day was beautiful and I always enjoy the sounds and smells of the Mustang. I took a bunch of pictures of Chloe on the way. As it turned out the sprinkler system in our yard came on as I was leaving so I stopped and took pictures of her with the water spraying in the background. If he picture below were in color you can see the rainbow caused by the water misting. Look just behind her collar. I don't know what that is going on at her neck, a thyroid goiter maybe or maybe a harbinger of things to come. Does she look sick or unhappy to you?

I stop at several stop signs and video Chloe looking around with the Beach Boys music playing in the background. *Darlin'* sounds so good in the Mustang. When we get to the vet I notice in front of their building adjacent to the parking lot is a red fire hydrant so I make a point to park in front of it and take advantage of the prop for a photo shoot. Chloe sits there very beautifully and I take several pictures just before taking her in for her evaluation.

Well Miss Chloe and I go into the vet's office to check her in. Already you begin to sense the anxiety experienced by every pet that is brought to this point. Despite the vet's personnel being polite and upbeat with their words and expressions it is a troubling time both for the owner of the pet and the pet being "dropped off." I hate it, I feel like I am disappointing the Chloe and betraying her somehow. The questions and paper work that accompanies the situation in addition to the looks you get from the pet is almost abstract to me. As usual however Chloe adapts to the impending change in her domicile for the moment and is not anxious at all and this gives some semblance of peace. Looking at her, she looked good and in good spirits but that tummy was just not right. It was bloated and big and not commensurate with her head or appendages. The attendant comes through the door after having being paged, "Chloe McHugh here for evaluation."

As she is leaving, another lady comes in with a pet and sees Chloe as she is going back. "What a pretty puppy," she says.

"Thank you, that she is and she is a very sweet dog too," I reply.

I turn to leave and smile as my eyes begin to water.

"She's still got it. She knows what she's doing," I thought to myself as I walked to the Mustang.

I have taken several thousand pictures of this most blessed creature and below is the last one I ever took and the last time I would ever see her alive.

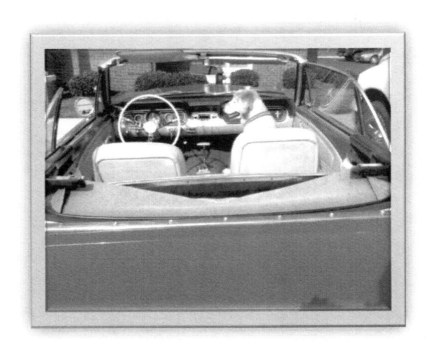

The Real Final Chapter
It's Meg all over again

John a doctor is finishing up with his afternoon patients when he hears the intercom, "Dr. McHugh line one please."

"She's gone John. Chloe's gone," Karen says crying.

"I was in the vet's waiting room to pick her up and they page me to the back as an emergency. They were getting Chloe out of the cage to bring her to me and she started bleeding and had a seizure. The vet wanted me to come back to witness what was happening to her because he thought she should be put to sleep. He asked me did I want to put her to sleep. It was terrible John seeing her like that. I was there to pick her up and bring her home. I can't bring her home. She is gone John. Chloe's gone."

Chloe was cremated and her ashes will be sprinkled about in the places she loved. Certainly a dash to the yards around our home and some at the cabins on the Chattahoochee River, but most will be reserved for that spot in the cove at the lake to left of the boat dock shaded by large Sycamores where she cooled off and bit at the water but never went under.

The End

And The Ends

Big Baby Girl a.k.a. Fiona

Baby Breeder a.k.a. Little Longfellow

The Dappled Evil Twins-Bree and Baby G

To be continued...

Ready for the lake:
The 86 Toyota truck
Chloe
Composter
Tomato cages
Blower
WeedEater
Mantis tiller
10-10-10
Cow Manure
Big Boy/Rutgers tomato plants
Wait a minute. What is that on the hood? Well that is our dachshund Tootsie eating cat food that my wife puts on the hood of the truck for our cat! No Tootsie, no more lake for you my little friend. Remember? Good try.

"John it has been two years since Chloe passed away. When
people ask about her what are you telling them?"

"That she's fine. I don't go there."

"John I don't think that's normal."

"I am sorry. I can't do it."